T0318835

LATIN AND ENGLISH IDIOM

LATIN AND ENGLISH IDIOM

AN OBJECT LESSON FROM
LIVY'S PREFACE

BY

H. DARNLEY NAYLOR, M.A.

Trinity College, Cambridge
Professor of Classics in the University of Adelaide

Cambridge:
at the University Press
1909

CAMBRIDGE
UNIVERSITY PRESS

University Printing House, Cambridge CB2 8BS, United Kingdom

Cambridge University Press is part of the University of Cambridge.

It furthers the University's mission by disseminating knowledge in the pursuit of
education, learning and research at the highest international levels of excellence.

www.cambridge.org
Information on this title: www.cambridge.org/9781316619933

© Cambridge University Press 1909

First published 1909
First paperback edition 2016

A catalogue record for this publication is available from the British Library

ISBN 978-1-316-61993-3 Paperback

TO THE BEST OF TEACHERS
AND TRUEST OF FRIENDS
STUART IVOR ATKINSON

PREFACE

THIS little book aims at giving the schoolboy and even the undergraduate assistance in acquiring Livian style. If the reader will cover the columns on the right hand side of chap. iii and then compare his version with that of Livy, he can have no ground of complaint, for he will have learnt a great amount of valuable Latin. But I venture to hope that he may find some of my comments useful.

I have referred in chap. i to a certain translation. I yield to no man in respect and admiration for the scholarship of its author, but experience has taught me that " accurate " versions are an unmixed evil. They ruin the English of the beginner, and are of no service to the advanced scholar. This fetich of " accuracy " begins at school with " which things having been done " and is continued, in a less flagrant form, even at our Universities. Two renderings should always be given whether in school or lecture-room: an " accurate " version (where explanation is necessary) and an English one. If this were done, the reproach would soon be wiped out that mediocre classical scholars are the worst writers of their own language.

For all that is erroneous or heterodox I am solely responsible; but my thanks are due to Professor T. G. Tucker of Melbourne University for help and criticism, and to Mr P. Giles of Emmanuel College, Cambridge, who has read through the proofs and saved me from more than typographical errors.

H. D. N.

ADELAIDE UNIVERSITY,
30 *October*, 1908.

CHAPTER I.

I have endeavoured in Chap. III. to treat Livy as he should be treated—as a fine writer of Latin Prose. Livy is neither an ideal historian nor antiquarian nor lawyer : but he is master of his own language, and the more closely one studies him, the more one realizes how magnificently he used his instrument.

In no way can we more clearly appreciate his power than in watching him deal, as it were, with our own language; and this has been my point of view throughout:—how would Livy put this or that into Latin or rather (I hope), how has he done it?

Every teacher is prompt to impress upon his pupils the value of re-translation from English versions into the dead languages; and every teacher is aware that pupils vastly prefer to put original English passages into Latin and Greek. The reason is very simple : in translating from Latin and Greek into English we adopt a totally different method from that which we use in the converse process. In the former case accuracy is made the principal, if not the sole, aim : the English is tolerably idiomatic, but any scholar of only limited experience can at once detect the form and method of the original. This is so true that one often observes in commentaries a note containing an accurate verbal rendering of some phrase ; this will be in inverted commas and passes for translation. Then the editor, somewhat naively, adds :

"*We say* so and so." For instance on the words ἤσθετο ἐκείνους
οὐ παρόντας ἔτι ἀλλ' ἤδη πεφευγότας your commentator may
remark : "*We say* ' he found that the bird had flown'." As if
" we say " and translation were different things. Whereas what
" we say " is of all things the *English* version of the original.
Unfortunately the case stands thus : if I give "he found that
the bird had flown" as my rendering of the above Greek, I shall
be condemned for a piece of impertinent paraphrase ; on the
other hand, if I am faced by the above English phrase and
serve up "ἤσθετο κ.τ.λ.," I shall be applauded for writing
idiomatic Greek. (See Sidgwick, *Lectures on Greek Prose*,
p. 42, § 4.)

There is obviously something not quite sound in the conventional attitude towards paraphrase. The methods of expression found in the two dead languages are often so utterly
different from those of modern times that we allow the impos-
sibility of word-for-word renderings from English, but make no
such concession when the position is reversed. Thus were I
asked to put into Greek " In this way the myth was preserved,"
I write οὕτως ὁ μῦθος ἐσώθη καὶ οὐκ ἀπώλετο; but your "translator"
says (Davies and Vaughan, *Plato Rep.* 621 B) : " thus...the tale
was preserved *and did not perish*." Yet surely it is for the
commentator to tell us how the phrase " goes " literally ; for the
translator to say it as an Englishman would have done. The
point is clearly illustrated by the following passage from a well-
known translation of Cicero's *Academics*. It is a typical
specimen of what is called " accurate" translation[1]. For ex-
amination purposes it is, doubtless, excellent, but, just because
the form of the original is so obvious, it is almost useless to the
re-translator. I italicize the points of interest and give footnotes
in justification of my changes for purposes of re-translation.

[1] The translator says in his Preface that "accuracy has been studied
rather than finish of style."

Cic. *Ac. Pr.* 2. 1. 3.

" Consequently so *great* [1] a general did he become in every department of the art of *war* [2], in battles, sieges, naval engagements, and the entire equipment of, and preparation for, *war* [3], *that* [4] the *greatest* [5] prince since Alexander admitted that he had found him to be a *greater* [6] leader than any one of those whose lives he had read. He also possessed *such* [7] skill in the organization and administration of states, and was *so just, that* [8] at the present day Asia persists in maintaining the ordinances of Lucullus and in almost following out his footsteps. But although the advantage to his country was great [9], still *such* [10] a high degree of excellence and ability was detained longer than I could wish in foreign parts, *far from the gaze of the forum and the senate.*" [11]

" *Tantus* [1] ergo imperator omni genere *belli* [2] fuit, proeliis, oppugnationibus, navalibus pugnis, totiusque *belli* [3] instrumento et apparatu, *ut* [4] ille rex post Alexandrum *maximus* [5] hunc a se *maiorem* [6] ducem cognitum, quam quemquam eorum, quos legisset, fateretur. In eodem *tanta* [7] prudentia fuit in constituendis temperandisque civitatibus, *tanta aequitas ut* [8] hodie stet Asia Luculli institutis servandis et quasi vestigiis persequendis.

Sed, etsi *magna* [9] cum utilitate reipublicae, tamen diutius quam vellem, *tanta* [10] vis virtutis atque ingeni peregrinata abfuit *ab oculis et fori et curiae.*" [11]

[1] [5] [6] [9]—This repetition of " great " is not only tolerable in Latin but actually idiomatic. Witness tantus, maximus, maiorem, tanta (prudentia), tanta (aequitas), tanta (vis). For [1] say " able " ; for [6] " finer," and the repetition is less offensive. The same criticism applies to [2] and [3]. In [2] substitute "military science" for " the art of war."

[4] [7] [8]—These long consecutive clauses are typical of Cicero, but one is enough in English. At [7] write " much " for " such," and at [8] write " as well as fair-mindedness. Indeed..." in place of " and was so just, that...." Beginners rarely remember that

such clauses (e.g. ita...ut) are often little more than equivalents
for "et" combining two principal verbs. I venture to think that
"stet" by its emphatic position = "stands firm." The "quasi"
may well be omitted in English: the metaphor is a common-place
one with us. I would therefore translate :—"Asia owes her
stability to maintaining the ordinances of Lucullus and to
following closely in his footsteps."

[10]—See note on [1] [5] [6] [9].

[11]—Here, perhaps, your translator cannot help himself. I
would merely say that were one required to put into Latin : "far
from our public and parliamentary life," "ab oculis et fori et
curiae" would be gratefully accepted by any examiner.

Need we be surprised that the student resents being set to re-
translate, and that he prefers exercising his talents on original
English passages?

The fact is we *Latinize* and *Grecize* (I dare not say "paraphrase"): we do not "translate." On the other hand we are
not allowed to *Anglicize*, for this would be to commit the un-
pardonable sin of paraphrasing. As specimens of Grecizing I
take a few random instances from Sidgwick's *Lectures on Greek
Prose*, p. 34, § 3, "in the agonies of death " = χαλεπῶς ἔχοντα ;
p. 47, § 6, "the stages of the farce having been first duly
arranged " = πάντα ἐς ἀπάτην παρασκευασάμενοι ; p. 48, § 7, "fell
into the trap" = ἐξαπατηθείς etc. These are all excellent Greek ;
but what would be said of the candidate who dared to render
this Greek into such English ! And yet the English version is
probably what an Englishman "would say."

At a time when Classics are on their defence it might be well
even to sacrifice "Composition" altogether, and ask our students
to "Anglicize" as well as "translate" the passages set before
them. I trust that Chap. III. will show how much educational
value can be got from this substitute for "Proses "; a value
which appears to me little inferior to the value of the old method

and is certainly superior in one point—that we save all the years spent on learning to avoid vulgar errors of grammar and syntax. For to write *accurate*, as distinguished from *idiomatic*, Latin and Greek is much more a matter of continual practice and a τριβὴ ἄλογος, than a sign that observation has been trained and a grand educational benefit conferred upon the suffering learner.

There is a further reason for dealing thus with our authors: in these days of elaborate editions where "notes" on points of archaeology, history, philology, orthography, textual criticism etc., etc., are heaped before the unhappy examinee, there is a real danger of his missing altogether the language itself. So true is this that in examinations where "Set Books" receive any prominence, the "mere translation" tends to take a quite secondary place. In fact minutiae loom too large in modern scholarship. We dwell at inordinate length on some question of reading or antiquities (who has not groaned over the Servian Constitution?) until we forget that Livy wrote a vast amount of Latin, of which by far the greatest part is perfectly clear and straightforward. Indeed, if all disputed passages were omitted, very little would be lost to history, and a great deal gained for literature.

CHAPTER II.

If I were asked :—What is *the* great feature of Livy's style ? I would boldly answer : "His brilliant use of order." I hope in Chap. III. to justify this criticism to some extent. I might have crowded my pages with hundreds of parallels in the matter of order, but mere references are, as a rule, of little value, while anything else would have caused this book to be "hampered by its own size."

I therefore content myself with pointing out principles which any student of ordinary ability can verify, and should verify, for himself. For details I would refer him to Professor Postgate's *Sermo Latinus*, pp. 35—45, but I venture to state again these few broad rules of *normal* Latin order :

(1) Subject 1st, Object next, Verb last; or Verb 1st, Object next, Subject last.

(2) Epithets of any kind (including the genitive case) immediately follow the word to which they belong, i.e. are "postpositive."

(3) Adjectives of number and quantity, demonstrative pronouns, and adverbs immediately precede the words to which they belong, i.e. are "prepositive."

(4) Co-ordinate and subordinate conjunctions, relative and interrogative pronouns or adverbs come first in their clause.

(5) A Latin sentence if *constructionally* complete must *ipso facto* be at an end.

Any departure from the normal order gives stress to the word in an abnormal position, e.g. a normally postpositive word has stress by being written prepositive and has still more by being separated from the word to which it belongs.

This then must be realized once and for all : *it is departure from the normal order that makes expressive Latin*.

Livy by his abnormalities, greater or less, can, I believe, express every nuance of modern English intonation. If we were to write a piece of Latin where every word should be piously placed in accordance with the above scheme of normal order, it would be as if an Englishman should read a passage in his own language without one new inflection or one change of intonation.

In the majority of cases Rule 1 holds good, though Livy may also write in the order of the picture as it comes on the screen, irrespective of the grammatical form. This he does with graphic effect in such passages as 1. 14. 8, and 44. 5. 6.

I would strongly urge that teachers should train their students to read Latin with stress on the words abnormally placed. For instance, "e terra ne gubernaveris" should be read with upward intonation on "e terra," just as we should read the italicized words in : "one should not steer a ship *from the land*." The immediate and complete grasp which the pupil gets of the writer's meaning will surprise those who have not made the experiment.

I hope to have shown that in almost all cases where an intelligent reader of English would use a changed intonation Livy has departed from the normal order in a greater or less degree.

Of course rhythm must be taken into account also ; but this is scarcely within the knowledge of Moderns, and in our own versions we can only hope for the best. Most of us may reasonably despair of writing Latin Prose at all if we are compelled to obey all the dicta of Professor Zielinski concerning " Das Clauselgesetz in Cicero's Reden " (*C. R.* Vol. xix. p. 164). Such researches will drive us all to seek refuge in the more satisfactory, because more certain, form of "composition" which I have ventured to name "Anglicizing."

The broad rules of Latin order stated above will, I trust, find ample and detailed illustration in the following chapter.

CHAPTER III.

α § 1. "Whether my efforts will be repaid if I write a complete history of the Roman people from the first foundation of the city, I neither know with any certainty, nor, if I knew, would I venture to say."

Facturusne operae pretium sim, si a primordio urbis res populi Romani perscripserim, nec satis scio, nec, si sciam, dicere ausim ;

"if I write a complete history of the Roman people."

"si…res populi Romani perscripserim."

β "Complete" is turned by "per" in "perscripserim"; cp. 35. 40. 1, "I have been led into a digression by this imbroglio of Greek and Roman *history*, not because the events themselves *deserved detailed treatment*, but because they brought about the war with Antiochus."

"Abstulere me velut de spatio Graeciae *res* immixtae Romanis, non quia ipsas *operae pretium* esset *perscribere*, sed quia causae cum Antiocho fuerunt belli."

γ Cp. 31. 1. 2, profiteri ausum perscripturum res omnis Romanas.

Cp. perpacare, perdomare, perpopulari, pervastare, perficere etc.

So 1. 56. 1, "to *complete* the building of temples."

"templa deum *exa*edificare."

a   "history of the Roman people"

Cp. § 3, p. 18, a, "the annals of a people..."

§ 6, p. 36, γ.   "The records of genuine history."

§ 10, p. 52, γ.   "Set in the conspicuous light of historic record."

22. 27. 3.   "The story has no historical authority."

β   7. 21. 6. "No history but knows their names."

Cic. *De Inv.* 1. 1, "when I begin to trace the events of historic narrative."

Cicero uses the word "historia" but not Livy, e.g. *De Leg.* 1. 1. 5, "Herodotus, the father of history";

and *Rep.* 2. 18, "the history

γ of Rome."   See Lewis and Short.

See § 2, "historians = scriptores," p. 16, a.

"from the first foundation"

The singular is rare)(§ 7, p. 38, δ, primordia.

Note "sciam ... ausim" — abnormal for "scirem...auderem," so the commentators. But there is no reason why Livy should not express it as a remote possibility.

δ   The form "ausim" for "audeam" occurs only in potential clauses and almost always with a negative.

§ 2.   "For I notice that this is a time-honoured and frequent practice, each new historian invariably believing that in his facts *he* will introduce something better authenticated, or in his elegant

---

"res populi Romani."

"rerum gestarum memoria... populi."

"incorrupta rerum gestarum monumenta."

"in illustri posita monumento."

"quod (=id quod) nulla memoria habet annalium."

"per omnium annalium monumenta celebres nominibus."

"cum res...ex litterarum monumentis repetere instituo."

"Herodotum, patrem historiae."

"Romana historia."

"a primordio."

"quippe qui cum veterem tum vulgatam esse rem videam, dum novi semper scriptores aut in rebus certius aliquid adlaturos se aut scribendi arte rudem vetustatem superaturos credunt."

a style will surpass the uncouth methods of early days."

"For I notice..."   "quippe qui...videam."

English makes a fresh start: Latin combines with the previous clause, using a relative whose causal sense is at once made clear by the particle "quippe." So in Greek the presence of ἅτε, ὡς, οἷα

β shows that the participle is causal; of καίπερ that it is concessive, and so on.

"practice"   "rem."

Cp. 26. 13. 9, "a long-established practice."   "vetus atque usitata res."

"in his facts"   "in rebus."

"Res" is the "blank cheque," of which the exact value can only

γ be discovered from the context. The following instances from Book I. will illustrate this:

§ 4, p. 22, γ. "Moreover it is an enormous undertaking.—*My history*..."   "Res est praeterea et immensi operis, ut quae..."

Cp. § 1, p. 10, a, "history of the Roman people."   "res populi Romani."

§ 10, p. 50, δ. "In the study of the *past*."   "in cognitione rerum."

δ   § 11, p. 59, β. "Absence of cupidity was proportioned to absence of its *objects*."   "quanto rerum minus, tanto minus cupiditatis erat."

§ 12, p. 64, γ. "The commencement of this great *task*."   "Initium tantae rei ordiendae."

1. 1. 4. "The inception of a greater *destiny*."   "maiora rerum initia."

1. 1. 10. "This *event* confirmed the Trojans in their hope."   "ea res Troianis spem adfirmat."

1. 2. 3. "Disheartened at their *position*."   "diffisi rebus."

α 1. 3. 1. "The Latin *kingdom*"

"res Latina."

1. 3. 3. "A flourishing city for those *days*."

"urbs florens ut tum res erant."

1. 6. 3. "Thus the Alban *throne* was given to Numitor."

"ita Numitori Albana re permissa."

1. 8. 6. "A new *environment*."

"novarum rerum."

1. 9. 1. "The *power* of Rome" (cp. 1. 2. 3).

"res Romana."

β 1. 13. 4. "Leaders and soldiery alike were touched by this *appeal*."

"movet res cum multitudinem tum duces."

1. 23. 4. "This *movement* roused Mettius from his inaction."

"ea res stativis excivit Mettium."

1. 36. 1. "The *attack* was so unexpected."

"adeo ea subita res fuit."

1. 37. 2. "This *success* struck
γ terror into the hearts of the Sabines as they fought, and also, when they were forced to retire, hampered their retreat."

"ea quoque res in pugna terrorem attulit Sabinis, et fusis eadem fugam impediit."

1. 37. 6. "In spite of their *failure*."

"quamquam *male gesta res* erat."

1. 40. 6. "One of them commenced his *tale*."

"unus rem...orditur."

1. 41. 3. "If this sudden
δ *horror* paralyse your brain."

"si tua re subita consilia torpent."

1. 46. 2. "The *incident* however did not diminish Tarquin's hopes" (cp. 1. 12. 10).

"neque ea res Tarquinio spem minuit."

1. 49. 2. "Whom he suspected of past leanings to the *régime* of Servius."

"quos Servii rebus favisse credebat."

1. 50. 8. "This *engagement* had taken up the whole day."

"ea res exemerat illum diem."

1. 51. 3. "Overcome by some startling *news*."

"re nova perturbatus."

α   1. 51. 4. "The *project* was postponed."

"dilatam rem esse."

1. 51. 7. "*Suspicion* was aroused by the impetuous spirit of Turnus."

"*suspectam* fecit *rem* ... ingenium Turni ferox."

1. 52. 2. "The whole Alban *empire.*"

"res omnis Albana."

1. 52. 4. "*Rome,*" i.e. the Roman empire.

"*res Romana.*"

β   1. 54. 3. "The Gabine *arms* were victorious."

"Gabina res superior erat."

1. 54. 10. "The Gabine *people*"

"Gabina res."

1. 55. 6. "The *world's* capital"

"caput rerum."

1. 55. 9. "For that *purpose*"

"in eam rem.",

1. 57. 3. "An *attempt* was made to see if..."

"*temptata res* est si..."

1. 59. 7. "The revolting *story* made no less an impression at
γ Rome."

"nec minorem motum animorum Romae tam atrox res facit."

It should be borne in mind that "res" is merely a somewhat extreme case of a general principle. Latin (like Greek) has comparatively few ornamental synonyms, and is not afraid of repeating a word. Variety of vocabulary, for mere variety's sake, is a modern
δ invention. See note § 4 on "what lies nearest these = proxima originibus," p. 25, γ.

"time-honoured"

"veterem."

Note that in strictness "vetus" = having existed a long time)("recens"=having existed a short time ; while "antiquus" merely means "having existed in the past")("novus" = never before existent, cp. p. 27, δ.

α   "believing"

This "dum" almost equals "quod."

Cp. Cic. *In Caec.* 17. 56, "In wishing to keep a few slaves, she lost her own liberty."

The use is frequent in Livy, cp. 3. 67. 6, etc. The construction is as with "dum" of "partial

β contemporaneity," i.e. the Pres. Indic. follows, no matter what the tense of the principal clause. Exceptions in Livy are 5. 8. 2, 5. 13. 13, 5. 25. 3.

Cicero has a similar use of "cum" followed by the Pres. Indic. (and, of course, a Present in the principal clause). Cp. *Rosc.*

γ *Amer.* 19. 54,

"In saying nothing of them, you admit that they do *not* exist." And in his letters we have passim : tibi gratulor *cum* vales = quod vales.

Livy uses this *cum* even with an historic tense, cp. 21. 18. 4.

"Your previous embassy show-

δ ed no less hastiness in demanding Hannibal for punishment."

"Each new historian invariably..."

Cp. 3. 66. 2, "novis semper certaminibus."

This position of the adverb between attribute and noun is typical of Livy and of poetry. Cp. Verg. *Georg.* 1. 319,

"far-spreading fields of ripening corn."

"dum...credunt."

"Dum pauca mancipia...retinere vult,...libertatem suam perdidit."

"ea...cum taces nulla esse concedis."

"praeceps vestra,..., et prior legatio fuit, cum Hannibalem... deposcebatis."

"novi semper scriptores."

"gravidam late segetem."

a   Here it is much like the Greek—οἱ ἀεὶ συγγράφοντες.

Usually the adverb will become an adjective or the equivalent in English. Thus—

1. 6. 2. "The *subsequent* murder of the tyrant."

" caedem deinceps tyranni."

1. 17. 4. "The many *surrounding* states."

" multarum circa civitatium."

β   1. 19. 4. "All the *neighbouring* nations."

" omnium circa finitimorum."

1. 21. 6. "Two *successive* kings."

" duo deinceps reges."

1 24. 1. "In both *those* armies"

" in duobus tum exercitibus."

1. 39. 3. "What will bring great honour *public* and *private*."

" materiam ingentis publice privatimque decoris."

1. 55. 9. "One city *of that period*."

" unius tum urbis."

γ   3. 2. 13. "Many *scattered* bands."

" multas passim manus."

We have a more careless order in 1. 19. 2, circa omnes populos,

and 1. 4. 4, "By some mysterious dispensation of Providence."

" Forte quadam divinitus."

1. 56. 9. "A symbolical representation of his character."

" Per ambages effigiem ingenii sui."

δ   A rarer construction, and therefore to be sparingly imitated, is :—

A.   No noun expressed—

1. 45. 1, formatis...omnibus domi.

1. 58. 2, satis tuta circa.

B.   No adjective or equivalent added—

3. 39. 4, deincepsque reges.

α   " historians "

So often in Livy, cp. 1. 59. 11,
" Not so easy for the historian to
reproduce," cp. p. 10, γ.

Cicero uses " historicus " but
not Livy. See § 1, " history = res,"
p. 10, α.

            " *he* "

Emphatic. The stress in En-
β glish is produced in Latin by
the order, i.e. " se," the subject,
is put after the verb, cp. 3. 13. 5,

" tribunus supplicium negat
sumpturum se de indemnato "
and 21. 1. 1 (me), 40. 57. 9 (se).

Contrast the normal order—

" se in rebus aliquid certius
adlaturos " with Livy's " in rebus
γ certius aliquid adlaturos se," and
observe that in the former we
lose :

(1) The stress on " in rebus."
This, as if with μέν, prepares the
way for " scribendi," which itself
has point because prepositive.

(2) The stress on " better authenticated " — " certius " is pre-
δ positive.

(3) The stress on " se," by
which the " novi scriptores " contrast their efforts with those of
predecessors.

            " elegant style "
)(" uncouth methods of early
days."

Hence " rudem " is prepositive
to point the antithesis with " arte,"
and makes a chiasmus.

" scriptores."

" Haudquaquam relatu scrip-
toribus facilia."

" scribendi arte."
" rudem vetustatem."

α   Observe that "credunt" comes last. Verbs of "saying, thinking, believing" etc. tend to come early, for what is "said, thought, believed" is the important thing. But if they have point, they come at the end. Here Livy has a sly hit at the "novi scriptores," who always *fancy* that they are going
β to surpass their predecessors. Cp. § 6, p. 35, β, "traduntur."

§ 3. "Still, whatever happen, I shall find pleasure—in having, to the best of my ability, played *my* part in doing justice to the annals of the leading nation of the world ; and if in such a cloud of historical witnesses my fame be
γ overshadowed, the renown and greatness of those who eclipse the writer's repute, should be his consolation."

"whatever happen," cp. 3. 2. 4.

"I shall find pleasure—"

The effect of the dash in English is to lay emphasis on the fact that Livy, in any case, will
δ have reaped enjoyment. This is done in Latin by putting "iuvabit" first.

"played *my* part in doing justice to."

The stress on "my" implies : "as well as others"—Greek καὶ αὐτόν.

Livy is the first of Roman writers to freely use "et" in all the meanings of καί. See p. 40, γ.

"Utcumque erit iuvabit tamen rerum gestarum memoriae principis terrarum populi pro virili parte et ipsum consuluisse ; et, si in tanta scriptorum turba mea fama in obscuro sit, nobilitate ac magnitudine eorum me, qui nomini officient meo, consoler."

"utcumque erit."

"et ipsum...consuluisse."

α   "consuluisse"—a sort of fut.
perf. infin. = "si consuluero."   Cp.
3. 33. 9, 3. 41. 3, and 3. 48. 3.   So
Ovid, *Heroides* 20. 52.

"the annals of the nation..."

Here "rerum gestarum memoriae" is practically one word and
therefore the following genitives
are inoffensive.

"rerum gestarum memoriae...
populi."

β   Cp. 1. 38. 1, "he was the
nephew of the king."   In this
phrase the order (i.e. genitives
on either side of the noun, as
in "rerum gestarum memoriae
populi") is almost invariable.   We
have an exception in 39. 11. 6,
"fratris eius filio."

"fratris filius erat regis."

It is a good rule to avoid a
γ double genitive if any ambiguity
be entailed.

"the leading nation of the
world."

Put what the English MEANS,
i.e. "a people head of the world."

Note that "orbis terrarum"
and "terrae" (not "terra") are the
prose phrases for "world."

"principis terrarum populi."

δ   "in such a cloud of historical
witnesses my fame be overshadowed."

"in tanta scriptorum turba
mea fama in obscuro sit."

The metaphor "cloud" is suffi-
ciently suggested by "in obscuro."
The stress on "my" is reproduced
by making "mea" prepositive, i.e.
"*my* fame")(the fame of my
rivals.

"In obscuro" instead of "obs-
cură" agreeing with "fama" is a

a common trick of Livy, perhaps borrowed from Greek (ἐν ἡδονῇ Thuc. 1. 99. 2, 2. 75. 5 and 8. 39. 4, ἐν ἀσφαλεῖ, Herodt. 7. 15, Eurip. *I. T.* 494. Also ἐν εὐμαρεῖ *I. A.* 969, ἐν ἀσφαλεῖ *Hipp.* 785, ἐν δίκῃ, ἐν αἰσχύνῃ κ.τ.λ.).

Cp. 2. 3. 1, "it was doubtful"   "in dubio erat."
3. 8. 9.   "They were easy"   "in facili erant."
3. 65. 11. "It is difficult"   "in difficili est."

β   The construction is most frequent with adjectives of the 2nd declension. See § 5 on "from the path of truth = a vero," p. 33, β.

"in such a cloud of historical witnesses."   "in tanta scriptorum turba."

The phrase is of course from Hebr. xii. 1. In such cases the student should ask himself what
γ the English really *means* stripped of all literary allusion. Here the *meaning* is "a crowd of historians."

Thus "the pearl of great price" becomes "unicum illud et inrevocabile" (H. N.).

"in tanta...turba"—"in"+abl. may express:
δ   (1) locality,
     (2) attendant circumstances,
     (3) "in the case of."

No. (2) is a very elastic use, and, like the Greek participle, the exact meaning is decided by the context. It may be (*a*) causal, as here; (*b*) concessive.

Observe (1) tanta, (2) scriptorum, (3) turba—the normal order, i.e. adjective, complement,

α noun. Nos. (1) and (3) may in-
terchange, but (2) is practically
invariable.

Cp. 2. 33. 7, "the buildings   "imminentia muro aedificia."
overhanging the wall," and see
§ 12, p. 61, δ, on "passion for
wasting oneself," etc.

"renown"   "nobilitas."

This noun and the adjective
β "nobilis" never express "noble"
in the moral sense. For this
Latin uses :

  ⎰probus ⎰probitas
  ⎱honestus, ⎱honestas.

The prevailing meanings of
"nobilitas" and "nobilis" are :
high-birth, fame, notoriety.

"eclipse the writer's repute"   "nomini officient meo."
γ "Writer's" is an "ornate alias"
for "my" .∴ "meo."

Note the position of "meo."
Livy is peculiarly fond of placing
a single word after the verb, more
especially one which scans ⌣ –.

Often, as here, when set after
the verb of a subordinate clause,
it prevents crowding of verbs at
δ the close of the sentence, cp. § 4
laboret sŭā, p. 24, a, § 5, p. 30, γ,
vidit aetas, § 9, p. 44, γ, intendat
animum and (p. 47, δ) sequatur
animo.

Furthermore there is stress on
"meo" as on "mea" in "mea
fama" above.

"eclipse"—   "officient."

The word "officere" in this
sense usually has a non-personal
subject.

α   Cp. 26. 40. 5, "the reputation he thus gained threw in the shade the fame of his commander-in-chief."

38. 58. 9. ne magnitudo et splendor legati laudibus consulis officeret.

1. 53. 1. "Had not degeneracy in other departments detracted β from his renown in this."

When the subject is personal use "obsto." Thus—

2. 33. 9. "The fame of Marcius overshadowed the consul's repute."

Cp. 26. 20. 3, "ne quis obstaret gloriae suae." "Obsto" is also used with a non-personal γ subject—

Cp. 1. 26. 5, "but the service so lately done palliated the offence."

officient—fut. For a future indicative inside a subjunctive clause referring to the future, cp. 2. 15. 3, 2. 29. 12. Cic. *Phil.* 2. 13. 32, 2. 44. 113, and *Acad. Prior.* 2. 7. 20, etc.

δ   eorum me qui—

Latin loves similar parts of speech crowded together, especially pronouns (cp. § 9, p. 42, β), and this separation of antecedent from relative is not uncommon, at least if *is* be the antecedent.

Cp. Cic. *Pro Leg. Man.* 12. 33, eius ipsius liberos qui...bellum gesserat; and Livy 1. 8. 3, me haud poenitet eorum sententiae

"Haec eius gloria imperatoris famae officiebat."

"Ni degeneratum in aliis (sc. rebus) huic quoque decori offecisset."

"Sua laude obstitit famae consulis Marcius."

"Sed recens meritum facto obstabat."

α esse, quibus etc. **33. 9. 8**, relicta ea parte suorum quae...vincebat. For separation of other antecedents than *is* cp. **1. 3. 8, 1. 8. 5, 1. 9. 14**, etc.

§ 4. "Moreover it is an enormous undertaking.—My history goes back more than seven centuries, and, starting from small β beginnings, has grown to such dimensions that now it is hampered by its own size. Further, the great majority of readers, I doubt not, will find less pleasure in first origins or what lies nearest these, and will hasten to those modern developments, whereby the might of an overgrown people γ has long been sapping its own strength."

"Moreover it is....—My history goes back..."

The second sentence is really an explanation of the first—my history is an enormous undertaking *because* it goes back....

δ   English leaves such things to the sense of the reader : Latin allows no excuse for stupidity and inserts "because" = ut quae.

Take a random instance in English, such as Prescott's *Mexico* **3. 3** :

"It was in vain the general called on them to close again and rally. *His voice was drowned* by the din of the fight," i.e. "because his voice" = quippe cuius vox....

"Res est praeterea et immensi operis, ut quae supra septingentesimum annum repetatur et quae ab exiguis profecta initiis eo creverit, ut iam magnitudine laboret sua ; et legentium plerisque haud dubito quin primae origines proximaque originibus minus praebitura voluptatis sint festinantibus ad haec nova, quibus iam pridem praevalentis populi vires se ipsae conficiunt."

"Res est praeterea..., ut quae ...repetatur."

α

"it...history"   "res."

See § 2, p. 11, β, "practice = rem."

"goes back more than seven   "supra septingentesimum an-
centuries."   num repetatur."

This *means* "goes back beyond
seven hundred years" — hence
Livy's Latin.

Cp. ὑπέρ in Thuc. 1. 41. 2, τὸν
ὑπέρ (before) τὰ Μηδικὰ πόλεμον.

β   "from small beginnings"   "ab exiguis profecta initiis."

Latin loves to suggest anti-
theses which to our minds seem
artificial.   Here the reader is
prepared for a contrast between
the small start and the great re-
sult by the separation of "exiguis" from its noun.

Similarly in "Res est"—res

γ has stress in antithesis to "scriptorum" in § 3 (p. 17).—That is, the
history and its length is a second
difficulty added to the large number of rivals in the field.

"and starting"   "et *quae*...profecta."

"et quae"—the relative is repeated because the *length* of the
history and its huge *growth* are

δ contrasted.   Cp. 38. 31. 5, qui
consuli M. Fulvio *quique* Romanis
Lacedaemonem dederent, where
qui...quique represent contrasted
parties.

"Such dimensions that" *means*
"to such an extent that"—hence
"eo—ut."

"is hampered by its own size"   "magnitudine laboret sua."

There is stress on "sua" by
separation, i.e. itself is a burden

α to itself. Also note "sŭā" after the verb and cp. § 3, p. 20, δ, "meo."

      "Further...majority..."

      "Further..."   "Et...."

This *et* answers to the *et* before immensi operis, which, like the formal "firstly," and like μὲν in Greek, merely tells us that a "secondly" is coming. Modern **β** English does not affect these anticipatory particles. Latin and Greek love to insert them. See note on § 6, p. 36, *a*, *β*, "better fitted = magis...."

Note that "both...and" (Greek τε...καὶ, μὲν...δὲ) = Latin et...et, cum...tum, tam...quam, ut...ita, qua...qua (epistolary).

γ "the great majority of readers"   "et legentium plerisque...."

"Readers" is the real subject and in Latin is made the logical subject by position, since it comes first, cp. §5, p.29, δ, 30, *a*, on"nostra."

The two points are—(1) The size of the work, (2) The readers and their ingratitude.

Therefore the stress is on **δ** "size" and "readers" and the adjective "immensi" and the genitive "legentium" are brought to the front.

      "readers"   "legentium."

This substantival use of the participle is especially common in the genitive plural. The singular also occurs, e.g. § 5, p. 33, *a*,   "scribentis animum." "the writer."

Other instances in Book I. are:

a   1. 8. 5. " Founders of cities "   " condentium urbes."
        1. 25. 4. " The spectators "   " spectantes."

Note that " of those reading"
= (1) legentium, (2) eorum qui
legunt = τῶν ἀναγιγνωσκόντων)(
" eorum legentium " which means
" of them while reading " = αὐτῶν
ἀναγιγνωσκόντων.

    " first origins *or* what lies   " primae origines proximaque
β nearest these."   originibus."

       " or " = " que."

Often " or " meaning " and as
the case may be " is translatable
by " que," as in Greek by καὶ
preceded by τε, or καὶ alone.

    Cp. § 9, p. 46, γ, " in war or peace "   " domi militiaeque."
    Cp. 1. 25. 3, " their nation's   " publicum (periculum) impe-
fate—empire or servitude."   rium servitiumque."

γ   Cp. 27. 45. 5, spem metumque,
34. 1. 4, ad suadendum dissua-
dendumque, and 34. 5. 1, etc.

    " what lies nearest *these* "   " proxima *originibus*."
    " these " = " originibus."

English abhors such repeti-
tions of the same word. In Latin
they are natural enough and especially frequent with the genitive
case, where English has a pronoun.

    Cp. 1. 7. 9, " listened to the   " facinus *facinorisque* causam
account of the crime and *its*   audivit."
excuse."

    3. 15. 8. " Daylight made clear   " lux deinde aperuit bellum
the nature of the war and the   ducemque *belli*."
identity of *its* leader."

    3. 72. 6. " But greed and *its*   " sed plus cupiditas et auctor
champion, Scaptius, won the day."   *cupiditatis* valet."

Instances of a different type are
seen in § 7, p. 41, *a*, "The nations of   " (ut) tam et hoc gentes hu-

a the world *acquiesce in* this with the same equanimity with which they *submit to* empire."

And § 9, p. 47, γ, "was *relaxed* …was *undermined.*"

1. 50. 6. "*Pay* as little *heed* to this day of meeting *as he does* who convened it."

1. 53. 4. "His attempts to **β** storm the neighbouring *city* of Gabii proved futile. A repulse from *its* walls robbed him further of the hope of a successful blockade. He finally," etc.

1. 59. 7. "The revolting story *made* no less an impression at Rome than it *had done* at Collatia." Compare 1. 46. 8 and 6. 34. 10.

γ   Of course Latin uses the "vicarious *facere*"—see Holden, *De Officiis* 1. 1. 4, as Greek δρᾶν (Thuc. 2. 49. 5) and ποιεῖν (Plato, *Rep.* 359 B).

It should be clearly understood that such repetition is a feature of Latin style, not a sign of weakness. Compare § 2 on "rem," p. 13, γ.

δ What might be thought extreme cases like 3. 43. 6, where "corpus" is repeated four times in as many lines, are, after all, not so very uncommon. A striking specimen is Ovid's *Her.* 10, ll. 5—21, where "somnus" occurs five times; "litus" thrice in six lines; and "torus" twice in three.

Also see Paley and Sandys, *Priv. Or.* Part i. (1898) 34 §§ 14

manae *patiantur* aequo animo quam imperium *patiuntur.*"

"labente…lapsi sint."

"neque magis *observaturos* diem concilii quam ipse qui indixerit *observet.*"

"Gabios propinquam *urbem* nequiquam vi adortus cum obsidendi quoque *urbem* spes pulso a moenibus adempta esset, postremo…."

"Nec minorem motum animorum Romae tam atrox res *facit* quam Collatiae *fecerat.*"

α and 18, and 35 § 18 (οἴνου...οἴνου ...οἶνον), and Jebb on Soph. *Antigone* l. 76.

"and will hasten"   "festinantibus."

Livy emphasizes their vulgar haste by writing "festinantibus ad haec nova" instead of "ad haec nova festinantibus." Notice that

β English starts a new sentence, connected by "and": Latin ties up with a participle, cp. on § 5, p. 32, δ, "and shall be free of every solicitude = omnis expers (ὣν) curae."

"modern developments"   "haec nova."

"modern" = "haec," cp. § 9, p. 50, α, "these modern days," and   "haec tempora."

1.55.9, "erections of modern times."   "(horum) operum."

γ   "developments" = "nova" (i.e. the civil war).

Note (1) the neuter plural often translates an awkward English noun—see § 5, p. 32, γ, on "those old times = prisca illa" and (p. 33, δ) on "from the path of truth = a vero." See p. 38, β.

(2) "nova" is more than "recentia" (see § 2, p. 13, δ, veterem)

δ which would be little better than a repetition of "haec." The word "novus" includes the notion of "unprecedented" like Greek νέος, νεώτερος. Cp. Horace's "nova monstra," and 1. 51. 3, "he professed to be overcome by some *startling news.*"   "quasi re nova perturbatus."

1. 56. 2. "These two works *all our modern* magnificence has scarcely been able to rival at all."   "quibus duobus operibus vix nova haec magnificentia quicquam adaequare potuit."

a   Here "all our" (ironical, cp.
"new-fangled") gives the force of
"nova." Livy thinks of the *por-
tentously* extravagant buildings
which were erected in his time.

"has so long been sapping"

"iam pridem…conficiunt."

By using the present (conficiunt) Livy shows that the process is still going on)(§ 5, "tot
β per annos vidit." Commentators
lay down that "iam pridem" must
be taken with "conficiunt," but
the order and the sense allow it
to be ἀπὸ κοινοῦ with "praevalentis" also.

§ 5. "I, on the other hand,
shall look to have this further
reward for my labours,—I shall
γ distract *my* attention from those
calamities which our generation
has lived to witness for so many
years, so long at least as I turn
all my thoughts back to those old
times ; and shall be free of every
solicitude which, while it cannot
divert a writer from the path of
truth, may yet prove a disturbing
δ influence."

" Ego contra hoc quoque laboris
praemium petam, ut me a conspectu malorum, quae nostra tot
per annos vidit aetas, tantisper
certe, dum prisca illa tota mente
repeto, avertam omnis expers
curae, quae scribentis animum
etsi non flectere a vero, sollicitum
tamen efficere posset."

"I, on the…attention…"

Note how the dash after
"labours" is translated by *ut*
"explanatory" — see Gild. and
Lodge, § 557, and Roby, § 1700.

"this *further*"

"hoc *quoque*."

"reward *for* my labours" in
Latin becomes "reward *of*…"

"laboris pretium.'

Only a genitive case can normally depend on a noun.

a　§ 7, p. 39, γ. "Renown *in* war"　　　"belli gloria."

Cp. § 11, 56, β, "affection *for* the work."　　　"amor negotii."

§ 12, p. 62, γ. "Passion *for* wasting oneself."　　　"desiderium pereundi."

§ 13, p. 66, a. "Supplications *to* gods."　　　"precationibus deorum."

The frequent "signum receptui" is an exception. Instances like Cic. *Leg.* 1. 15. 42, "obtempe-
β ratio scriptis legibus populorum" are very rare. Cp. Liv. 23. 35. 7, exprobratio cuiquam, 26. 19. 8, miraculis fides. Caes. *B.C.* 1. 5. 5, postulatis responsa; Cic. *Top.* 5. 28, traditio alteri.

"I shall distract *my* attention"　　　"me...avertam."

"my" has stress because "me" is *brought forward*, while the first
γ "I" is emphatic by *insertion* of "ego." Contrast the weakened effect had Latin omitted "ego," and written "ut a conspectu...me avertam."

"which our generation has lived to witness for so many years."　　　"quae nostra tot per annos vidit aetas."

Cp. Tac. *Hist.* 1. 43, Insignem illa die virum Sempronium Den-
δ sum aetas nostra vidit.

Weissenborn considers the order "freer and more poetic than that of earlier writers."

There is, at least, a tolerable explanation, if not a complete justification. Let us contrast the normal order—"quae aetas nostra per tot annos vidit."

In Livy's order "nostra" gets stress by separation. It contains the real subject, i.e. "nos ipsi"—

α we ourselves. Then, next in order of painfulness, comes the duration of it all, with stress on "tot" by separation, cp. 5. 21. 7, tot per dies, 10. 25. 18, quot per duces*; and, lastly, "vidit" is slightly emphasized by position, so as to equal ἐφορᾶν = "live to see," cp.

β 1. 46. 8 and 6. 34. 10, domi se... *visuram* regnum fuisse, 21. 53. 5, quantum ingemiscant patres nostri, ...si *videant* nos...in media Italia paventes. (The Romans regarded ancestors as still existing, cp. Ov. *Her.* 4. 161, miserere priorum.)

Finally comes "aetas" which, (1) re-echoes "nostra," suggesting
γ "in our life-time"; (2) comes last (a) because the order "nostra per tot annos aetas" would mean : "our life which has lasted for so many years"; (b) because Livy is peculiarly fond of a single word after the verb. See § 3, p. 20, δ, "meo."

For "nostra," logical subject (=nos ipsi) put first, cp. 44. 5. 2,
δ "An enemy could scarcely have produced a greater panic than did the elephants."

"hostilem prope tumultum... elephanti praebebant."

Pref. § 3, p. 17, γ. "The renown and greatness of these should be my consolation."

"nobilitate ac magnitudine eorum...me consoler."

In the following the *grammatical* subject takes a very humble place :

§ 9, p. 45, γ. "The qualities which won...the empire."

"quibus artibus...partum...imperium sit."

* Cp. Cic. *In Cat.* 1. 7. 16, Quis te...tot ex tuis amicis...salutavit ? and for the normal *per tot annos* cp. Livy, 26. 35. 5 and 26. 40. 11.

α   Cp. 3. 62. 2, "the tactics of my colleague and the bravery of the soldiers won the day."

§ 11, p. 56, a. "Still unless I be deceived by affection for the work I have undertaken."

1. 25. 6. "The Roman troops were now utterly disheartened."

β   32. 34. 6. "Because I am driven to undertake this war" (cp. 3. 68. 9, sed me vera pro gratis loqui...necessitas cogit), so Cic. *Ad Fam.* 6. 10. 4, "I am told...how you find strength and comfort in a conscience satisfied with its actions and motives."

γ   [Note that the order, in the last four instances, prevents any sense of harshness arising from the use of an abstract subject to a transitive verb. 1. 7. 5, cum eum cibo vinoque gravatum sopor oppressisset, 1. 7. 15, ad quam (immortalitatem) eum sua fata ducebant, 2. 40. 4, nisi me frustrantur oculi. Cp. 3. 49. 8, ne quid Verginii adventus in exercitu motus faceret, 7. 25. 13 (cp. 31. 18. 8), quos rapto vivere necessitas cogeret, 10. 41. 1, Romanos ira, spes, ardor certaminis...in proelium rapit; Samnitium magnam partem necessitas ac religio invitos...resistere...cogit, 22. 60. 2, feminas quoque...necessitas in foro turbae virorum immiscuerat.

δ

Of course an abstract subject

"consilio collegae, virtute militum victoria parta est."

"ceterum aut me amor negotii suscepti fallit, aut...."

"Romanas legiones iam spes tota...deseruerat."

"quia me necessitas ad hoc bellum...avertit."

"audiebam ... quam te vehementer consolaretur conscientia factorum et consiliorum tuorum."

α may always govern an abstract object in the accusative case.]

Cp. also 1. 1. 4, "a similar disaster exiled him from his home."

"ab simili clade domo profugum." Observe Livian "ab"= "by reason of."

1. 4. 6. "The basket, in which the children were exposed, floated, but, with the water of little depth on the parched ground, was soon β left stranded."

"cum fluitantem alveum, quo expositi erant pueri (note single word after the verb), tenuis in sicco aqua destituisset."

1. 5. 6. "Fear made him disclose the facts to Romulus."

"metu subactus Romulo rem aperit."

8. 21. 3. "This spirited reply, as the consul saw, only increased the opposition of those already hostile to the cause of the Privernates."

"Cuius cum feroci responso infestiores factos videret consul eos qui ante Privernatium causam impugnabant...."

42. 58. 4. "The numerous γ cries, the rush from the gates, put an end to all doubts."

"Plurium clamore et cursu a portis dubitatio exempta est."

"those old times"

"prisca illa."

The neuter plural translates "times"—see note on § 4, p. 27, γ, "modern developments = haec nova."

Priscus like *pristinus* has the additional idea of "old-fashioned." Thus "the good old days" would δ be "prisca illa tempora")("haec nova tempora."

"and shall be free of evéry solicitude."

"omnis expers curae.'

There is stress (upward intonation in English) on "omnis" by separation; cp. § 10, p. 52, β, "omnis te exempli documenta."

expers, sc. ὦν : English starts a fresh sentence connected by "and": Latin ties up with the

α participle, cp. § 4, p. 27, β, "festinantibus."

    "the writer"   "scribentis animum."

    Cp. § 4, p. 24, δ, "readers = legentium."

    Notice "animum" inserted. The word is not required in English, but is a commonplace of Latin. *The* point is the writer; therefore "scribentis animum,"
β not "animum scribentis."

    "from the path of truth"   "a vero.'

    In such phrases as "path of right, justice, truth," etc., the words "path of" are conventional. The metaphor is dead, cp. 62, γ. Hence "a recto, iusto, vero," etc., are quite adequate translations.

    Cp. § 12, p. 62, γ, "in the path
γ of luxury = per luxum."

    Note the neuter singular of adjectives in -us used to form nouns, mainly abstract. Compare English "from the blue," "out of the wet." So Livy 1. 4. 6, "on   "in sicco." the parched ground."

    See also § 3, p. 18, δ, "in obscuro," where Livy is seen to extend
δ the use to adjectives in -is. He even has the latter in the genitive case if combined with an adjective in -us. Cp. 5. 3. 9, "si quicquam in vobis non dico civilis, sed humani esset." So 42. 47. 9.

    Often, as I have pointed out, (§ 4, p. 27, γ, "developments = nova," § 5, p. 32, γ, "those old times = prisca illa," cp. § 6, p. 35, *a*, *a* "the events which=quae") the neuter plural of an adjective will do the work of awkward English nouns and abstract ideas. Thus Sallust, *Catiline*, Ch. 5—

"His mind lusted after the extravagant, the monstrous, the unattainable."

"animus immoderata, incredibilia, nimis alta cupiebat."

Cp. § 10, p. 54, γ, on "examples
β to imitate=quod imitere."

"may yet prove a disturbing influence."

"sollicitum tamen efficere posset."

Put what the English *means* in its simplest form, i.e. "may yet be able to make him anxious."

Note "efficere" for the more usual "facere." "posset" (v. l. possit)—an "impossible" apodo-
γ sis, whose protasis lurks in "expers curae," implying "if he had not been free from solicitude."

§ 6. "The events which, according to tradition, preceded the project⎫
completion or process⎭ of the city's foundation, are better fitted for the poet's romance than for the
δ records of genuine history, and it is no part of my plan to establish or refute them."

"Quae ante conditam condemdamve urbem poeticis magis decora fabulis quam incorruptis rerum gestarum monumentis traduntur, ea nec adfirmare nec refellere in animo est."

A valuable paragraph. Contrast the form as a whole in both languages. English has two sentences connected by "and," viz. "the events...are fitted...and I shall not...refute them." Latin says: "I shall not refute those events which are fitted" but in a *a* characteristic order, i.e. " what events are fitted, those I shall not refute." Cp. " who steals my purse, (he) steals trash."

"The events which..."   " quae."

The neuter plural to translate the noun of English. See § 5, p. 33, *β*, " from the path of truth = a vero."

" according to tradition "   " traduntur."

β   Probably there is slight stress on the verb, cp. § 2, p. 17, *a*, " credunt."

" preceded the completion or project ⎫ of the city's foundation " process ⎭   " ante conditam condendamve urbem."

The gerundive at times does the work of a present or future participle passive.

For the latter, cp. 21. 21. 8.

γ   " Between the sufferings of the past and those of a near future."   " Inter labores aut iam exhaustos aut mox exhauriendos (ἐξαντλεῖν)."

Observe how abstract nouns may be turned, (1) by the gerundive, cp. 1. 1. 1, "advocates of Helen's *restoration*" (with stress on " restoration ")(" retention."   " reddendae Helenae auctores."

δ Hence "reddendae" is prepositive).

(2) by the perfect participle passive. This is a commonplace in Livy, and is very frequent in the nominative. We get two types : (*a*) with a personal subject, e.g. 1. 34. 3, " Lucumo's pride was only increased by his marriage with Tanaquil."   " Lucumoni ... animos auxit ducta in matrimonium Tanaquil."

" *only* increased " is translated by stress on " auxit " placed early.

α   (*b*) with a non-personal subject, e.g. 1. 14. 9, "their alarm was re-doubled by a movement from the camp."

"addunt pavorem mota e castris signa."

Here "addunt" would poorly represent "redoubled" were it not put first in the sentence.

"better fitted" *means* "*more* fitted"; therefore

"magis decora."

β   Observe the separation of "magis" from "quam." So "prius... quam," "ante...quam," "potius... quam," etc. Latin loves such anticipatory orders—cp. ita...ut, adeo...ut, illud...ut (ἐκεῖνο...ὅτι, τοῦθ' ὅτι), idcirco...quod, etc.

See also § 4, p. 24, *a*, on "further=et," and § 9, p. 44, γ, "to the (life)...=ad illa," and § 12,

γ p. 63, δ, "painful enough even when=ne tum quidem gratae futurae cum..."

"better fitted for the poet's romance than for the records of genuine history."

"poeticis magis decora fabulis quam incorruptis rerum gestarum monumentis."

"poeticis," separated from its noun and prepositive, prepares us for the antithesis "incorruptis

δ monumentis"—cold, prosaic records.

Note how the generic adjective takes the place of the English noun. Thus "the fears of a woman"=

"muliebris timor."

Cp. 1. 47. 10, "usurped the throne a woman gave him."

"muliebri dono regnum occupasse."

And "it was *done* with the courage of a man, but the thoughtlessness of a child."

"acta illa res est animo virili, consilio puerili." Cic. *Att.* 14. 21. **3**.

a   Cp. 44. 5. 2, "panic produced by an enemy."

"decorus" with dat., cp. 2. 24. 5, 36. 14. 5.

For the whole phrase compare Prescott's *Mexico*, Pref. p. 8—

"(The subversion of a great empire by a handful of adventurers) *has the air of romance*
β *rather than of sober history* = ea omnia videntur poeticis magis decora esse fabulis quam incorruptis rerum gestarum monumentis."

Thus "a romantic adventure" would be: "res poeticis decora fabulis."

§ 7. "We do not deny antiquity the licence of mixing
γ human and divine elements to lend a greater dignity to a nation's earliest days; indeed, if any people may add an odour of sanctity to their origin, and trace it to a divine authorship, that people is the people of Rome; whose renown in war is such that, when they choose to represent
δ Mars as the father of themselves and of their founder, the nations of the world acquiesce in this with the same equanimity with which they submit to our empire."

"We do not deny antiquity the licence..."

"We do not deny" = "we give")("we refuse," i.e. there is stress on "give." Thus "datur" comes first.

"hostilem tumultum."

"Datur haec venia antiquitati, ut miscendo humana divinis primordia urbium augustiora faciat; et si cui populo licere oportet consecrare origines suas et ad deos referre auctores, ea belli gloria est populo Romano, ut, cum suum conditorisque sui parentem Martem potissimum ferat, tam et hoc gentes humanae patiantur aequo animo, quam imperium patiuntur."

"Datur haec venia antiquitati."

a   "the licence of mixing"   "venia...ut miscendo...[faciat]."
This means "this licence name-
ly that it may mix..." The "ut"
is "explanatory" (see p. 28, δ), and
a concessive subjunctive follows,
as after "licet ut."

Observe that the explanatory
genitive of English may be turned
by explanatory *ut* in Latin. Here
β "haec" is anticipatory—see § 6,
p. 36, β, on "better fitted = magis...
quam."

"human and divine *elements*"   "humana divinis."
Again the neuter rids us of an
awkward substantive. See § 4,
p. 27, γ, "developments = nova."

"lend a greater dignity to"
means "make more dignified"
—therefore   "augustiora faciat."

γ   "a nation's earliest days"   "primordia urbium.'
urbium—because the "nation"
of oldest time, of which Livy
thinks, was the πόλις, the *urbs*
Roma, not the imperium Roma-
num.

"nation," if civilized, is "popu-
lus" (not "populi" = peoples, com-
δ munities, nationalities) or "civitas."

On the other hand "nationes"
and "gentes," so frequently with
"exterae," suggest foreigners, βάρ-
βαροι, and often half-civilized
people.

primordia—the usual plural
)(§ 1, p. 10, γ, primordio.

"add an odour of sanctity to"   "consecrare."
A mere conventional phrase.
The metaphor is dead. What it

α *means* is "to make as if sacred " =
"consecrare."

There is a slight stress on
"consecrare," which precedes its
object, and this stress is echoed
in the following clause at the words
"ad deos referre auctores," as if
"ad *divinam* referre originem."

"trace it to a divine author-   " ad deos referre auctores."
β ship."

Note how "authorship"—ab-
stract—may be translated by
concrete "auctores."

"that people is the people of   "populo Romano."
Rome"

The position of "populo Romano" at the end of its clause
brings back to the mind "si cui
γ populo..." at the beginning of the
protasis.

"whose renown in war is   "ea belli gloria est ut..."
such..."

Note the frequent use of *is*
= talis. Also observe "*in* war" =
Latin genitive, cp. § 5, p. 28, δ,
"reward *for* labours = laboris pretium." There is stress on "belli"
δ prepositive, preparing us for the
claim of descent from the War-
god.

"as the father of themselves   "suum conditorisque sui pa-
and of their founder..."   rentem."

"suum" is prepositive and
separated from its noun, and so
has the effect of a dative of advantage, as if "claim for themselves
and their founder a parent in
Mars."

α   Similarly in Greek a possessive genitive takes the place of an ethical dative, especially if an enclitic brought forward at the beginning, cp. Plato, *Phaedo*, 117 A, ch. 66, ἕως ἄν σου (= σοι) βάρος ἐν τοῖς σκέλεσι γένηται, i.e. until *you find* your legs heavy.

     Further "conditoris" naturally
β comes next because parallel in sense to "suum," as if "suum" were a genitive case, i.e. "the parent (1) of themselves (suum), (2) of their founder (conditoris sui)." For (1) Livy could have written "sui" objective genitive, but the succeeding "sui" would have been very awkward.

γ   "the nations of the world"   "gentes humanae."

     Cp. § 7, p. 38, γ, above on "a nation's earliest days = primordia urbium."

       "in this"   "et hoc."

     Greek καὶ τοῦτο, cp. § 3, p. 17, δ, "*my* part = et ipsum."

     "acquiesce in this with the same equanimity with which they submit to our empire."   "et hoc...patiantur aequo animo, quam imperium patiuntur."

δ   "equanimity"   "aequo animo."

     The noun "aequanimitas" does not appear in good prose. Perhaps "securitas" is the nearest "classical" equivalent.

     There is stress on the adverbial "aequo animo" coming after its verb; the effect is an afterthought —"they acquiesce and with perfect equanimity too." Also it is α an ἀπὸ κοινοῦ position which thus allows the phrase to qualify both verbs.

In "aequo animo" the adjective is necessarily prepositive because "aequo" not "animo" is *the* point.

On "patiuntur" followed by "patiantur")(English "acquiesce in…submit to," see § 4, p. 25, γ,

β "what lies nearest these=proximaque originibus."

§ 8. "Still, this and the like, however criticised or appreciated, I, for my part, shall count of no great moment;"

"this and the like"

Greek τοιαῦτα καὶ παραπλήσια.

In Cicero similis (dissimilis)

γ takes genitive of the *person*, and genitive or dative of the *thing*, but always "veri simile" and "hoc simile est illi" (neut. pron.). For "hoc simile est illius" would mean: "this is like him."

Livy first has "vero simile," e.g. 8. 26. 6, 10. 26. 13, but it is rare. "veris simile" is more fre-

δ quent, e.g. 5. 21. 9 and passim. He also, at times, uses the dative of the person, e.g. 3. 65. 9, similes Icilio.

"I for my part shall count of no great moment."

"magno" has stress by separation.

"equidem," cp. οὐ περὶ πολλοῦ ἔγωγε ποιοῦμαι.

"Sed haec et his similia, utcunque animadversa aut existimata erunt, haud in magno equidem ponam discrimine;"

"haec et his similia."

"haud in magno equidem ponam discrimine."

α   "haud." See Gild. and Lodge, § 443, Note 3, and Roby § 2229.

Livy uses *haud* freely as a mere variant for *non*. Cicero restricts it to adverbs and adjectives (not already negatived or quasi-negatived) and with verbs only employs it regularly with *haud scio an*. He has sporadic

β instances of *haud ignoro*, *haud dubito*, and *haud erravero*.

§ 9. "rather I would have each give his undivided attention to the life and civilization of the past; the deeds of great men, the qualities in war or peace which won and added to the empire; then, as the tone of morality was

γ gradually relaxed, I would have him follow, in his mind's eye, the first sinking, as it were, of national character; next, how further and further it was undermined; how then it began its headlong career, until these modern days are reached, when neither our moral diseases nor their cures are

δ endurable to us."

"rather I would..."

"rather" is expressed by the adversative asyndeton. Cp. § 12, p. 60, δ, "*but* of late=nuper."

This is most common where the second clause has the negative, see Madvig's Grammar, § 458 (*a*) Obs. 1, where he quotes Cicero's "haec morum vitia sunt, *non* senectutis," and distinguishes "et

"ad illa mihi pro se quisque acriter intendat animum, quae vita, qui mores fuerint, per quos viros quibusque artibus domi militiaeque et partum et auctum imperium sit; labente deinde paulatim disciplina velut desidentes primo mores sequatur animo, deinde ut magis magisque lapsi sint, tum ire coeperint praecipites, donec ad haec tempora quibus nec vitia nostra nec remedia pati possumus, perventum est."

α non" and "ac non"="and not rather."

But adversative asyndeton is not infrequent where the first proposition is negatived as in the text.

Cp. 1. 17. 1, "as yet no single individual was infected with these feelings. Among the two nationali-
β ties, however, there was a keen party contest."

"necdum ad singulos (res) pervenerat : factionibus inter ordines certabatur."

1. 25. 3. "Neither bethought them of the danger, only of their nation's fate—empire or servitude."

"nec his nec illis periculum suum, publicum imperium servitiumque obversatur animo."

1. 47. 10. "Without confirmation by the patricians he had usurped the throne a woman gave him."

"non auctoribus patribus muliebri dono regnum occupasse."

γ   Cp. 3. 19. 3, 3. 32. 5, etc.

"I would have each..."

"mihi pro se quisque..."

"mihi"—ethical dative, allied to the dative of advantage. So in Greek: "please call the witnesses"=κάλει μοι τοὺς μάρτυρας.

"each"

"pro se quisque."

In prose, with rare exceptions,
δ quisque does not stand in a PRINCIPAL *clause* unless supported by (1) a distributive—as here—*pro se*, or by "suus," e.g. *suum* quisque (locum habet); by (2) "unus" as *unus*quisque; (3) in phrases such as *optimus* quisque, *quotus* quisque, *tertio* quoque anno. But we find it standing alone where quisque also stands in the subordinate clause, e.g. *De Off.* 1. 7. 21, quod cuique obtigit, id quisque teneat.

α   In the *subordinate* clause it is
regular by itself.   Contrast our
idiom in such cases, e.g. 22. 4. 6,
"each came down by the nearest
path."

"(milites) qua cuique proxi-
mum fuit, decucurrerunt."

"give his undivided attention"

"acriter intendat animum."

Observe that the epithet of
English becomes adverb in Latin,
and the noun verb, cp. Cic: *Brut.*
β 56. 205, "he had a *scholarly ac-
quaintance* with our early history
and literature." This is even more
common in Greek, cp. Thuc.
6. 33. 6.

"antiquitatis nostrae et scriptorum veterum *litterate peritus.*"

"After the unexpected but
signal defeat of the Mede."

τοῦ Μήδου παρὰ λόγον πολλὰ
σφαλέντος.

Cp. p. 48, β, "sinking = desidentes...headlong career = ire prae-
γ cipites."

Note how "intendat" precedes
"animum" because "attention"
is the point. In any case Livy
affects the single word after the
verb. See § 3, p. 20, δ, "meo."

"to the (life)..."

"ad illa..."

Latin loves these anticipatory
words (cp. Greek ἐκεῖνο δεῖ σκο-
δ πεῖσθαι). See note on § 6, p. 36, *a,*
"better fitted = magis..."

"life and civilisation of the
past."

"quae vita, qui mores fuerint."

Or "private life and public
morals..."

For "mores" see p. 48, β,
"national character = mores."

"And" is expressed by anaphora (quae...qui). This straining
after oratorical effect is typical of

α all Latin. See § 10, p. 54, δ, on "re-pulsive from first to last = foedum inceptu, foedum exitu" and cp. the artificial contrasts in § 4,'p. 23, β, note on "small beginnings."

　　　　"of the past"　　　　　　　"fuerint."

　　Cp. 1. 49. 2, "whom he sus-pected of *past leanings* to the régime of Servius."　　　　"quos Servi rebus *favisse* cre-debat."

β　　"the deeds of great men, the qualities in war and peace which won and added to the empire."　　　　"per quos viros, quibusque artibus domi militiaeque et par-tum et auctum imperium sit."

　　It is well to avoid abstract nouns as subjects to transitive verbs. Therefore write, not "what qualities won the empire," but, "by what qualities the empire was won." The order is as if γ "artes" were subject. See note on § 5, p. 30, γ, "nostra...vidit aetas."

　　"the deeds of great men" = "per quos viros," i.e. δι' ὧν)("the great men who won" = "a quibus viris," i.e. ὑφ' ὧν.

　　　　"qualities"　　　　　　　"artibus."

　　The word "artes" in Cicero and Caesar is almost exclusively δ used of intellectual accomplish-ments. But elsewhere, especially with "bonae" or "malae," it ex-presses moral qualities.

　　Cp. Sall. *Cat.* ch. 5, "both these he had increased by the qualities to which I have already alluded."　　　　"quae utraque his artibus aux-erat quas supra memoravimus."

　　In Livy I. we have the following various shades of meaning :—

　　1. 39. 4. "He was educated　　"erudiri artibus quibus ingenia

α in all those *branches* which inspire the character to fill a high place in the world."

ad magnae fortunae cultum excitantur."

1. 39. 4 (ad fin.). "There was not one among the young men at Rome who could be compared with Servius in any single *accomplishment.*"

"nec quisquam Romanae iuventutis ulla arte conferri potuit."

1. 50. 7. "This man of faction β and turbulence who had won influence in his own home by like *methods.*"

"seditiosus facinorosusque homo eisque artibus opes domi nactus."

1. 53. 1. "Indeed his *skill* as a general would have ranked him with his predecessors on the throne."

"quin ea arte aequasset superiores reges."

1. 53. 4. "He finally adopted *tactics* wholly un-Roman in the γ shape of deceit and treachery."

"postremo minime arte Romana fraude ac dolo aggressus est."

"in war or peace"

"domi militiaeque."

For "que" = "or" see § 4, p. 25, β, on "first origins or what lies nearest these = primae origines proximaque originibus."

For the phrase cp. Prescott's *Mexico*, Bk II. ch. 7, "the stomach —that great laboratory of disaffec-δ tion, whether *in camp or capital.*"

"won and added to the empire"

"et partum et auctum imperium sit."

Observe that "partum" and "auctum" are put early because "won" and "added to" is the point, and therefore deserves stress.

et...et..., natural to Latin, but stiff and archaic in English.

"then as the tone of morality was gradually relaxed..."

"labente deinde paulatim disciplina..."

a   First notice how "labente" precedes the connective "deinde." It tickets, as it were, the new section. The materials with which to build up the empire have been obtained (partum); the building has been erected (auctum); and now comes the undermining (labente) of the structure.

β   "disciplina" includes the two ideas of teaching and discipline. Without an epithet it often implies the education of stern old times, but epithets are added in

1. 18. 4. "The stern and severe school in which the Sabines of old were trained."

"disciplina tetrica ac tristi veterum Sabinorum."

[N.B. The word "tetricus" γ is marked "tĕtrĭcŭs" in L. and S., but both their quotations from Ovid show it to be a short "e."]

"relaxed"   "labente."

but below "was undermined"   "lapsi sint."

For the repetition in Latin see § 4, p. 25, γ, on "what lies nearest these."

"I would have him follow in his mind's eye."

"mihi...sequatur animo."

δ   "animo" by position becomes an afterthought = "follow it—that is mentally." Also it illustrates Livy's fondness for a single word after the verb, see § 3, p. 20, γ, "meo."

"the first sinking, as it were, of national character; next, how further and further it was undermined; how then it began its headlong career..."

"velut desidentes primo mores (sequatur animo), deinde ut magis magisque lapsi sint, tum ire coeperint praecipites..."

a There is stress on "sinking" in English, contrasted with the gradually increased rate of downfall. This is why "desidentes" comes first. The next step is "magis magisque lapsi"; the last "ire praecipites," where "praecipites" is put last in antithesis to "desidentes."

Notice how the abstract ideas,
β —"sinking," "headlong career"—become verbs. Cp. p. 44, *a*, on "give his undivided attention = acriter intendat animum."

  "national character"   "mores."

  "mores" may refer to communities as well as to individuals. Cp. p. 44, δ, "civilisation of the past = qui mores fuerint."

γ Observe in this passage the metaphors from falling buildings —"labente ... desidentes ... magisque lapsi...ire praecipites...vitia (cp. p. 50, *a*)..."

Such metaphors are frequent in Livy, though unnatural in English. Thus 8. 7. 19,

  "Military discipline is *at an*
δ *end* through your act: your punishment must *restore* it."

  "disciplinam militarem culpa tua *prolapsam* poena tua *restituas*."

  36. 6. 2. "The high tone of morality which once distinguished the people became *relaxed*."

  "*labante* egregia quondam disciplina gentis."

Cp. the frequent "pugnam *restituere*" (e.g. 4. 38. 5) where we should say "to *rally* the fight."

Cp. also 23. 45. 3,

  "The strong body and spirit *are no more*." So we say (but with

  "*dilapsa* esse robora corporum animorumque."

a less dignity) : "his courage went to pieces."

    45. 19. 9. "The cause, almost *lost*, was saved by him."

    Tumbling buildings were only too common in Rome, as Juv. 3. 193 shows, "nos urbem colimus tenui tibicine fultam magna parte sui"; but we have Municipal

β Councils, and this is one of the metaphors which English must either drop altogether or expand into a simile. [Far more common, of course, is the converse, i.e. a Latin simile introduced by tamquam, quasi, etc. will disappear in an English metaphor. Thus 3. 34. 7, *velut* corpus omnis

γ Romani iuris="the whole body of Roman law." Cic. *Acad. Prior.* 2. 1. 3, *quasi* vestigiis persequendis = "by following closely in his footsteps."]

    Prescott's *Mexico*, Bk II. ch. 6, well illustrates what I have just pointed out :—

    "Thus, the more widely the

δ Aztec Empire was extended, the weaker it became; RESEMBLING *some vast and ill-proportioned edifice*, whose disjointed *materials*, having no principle of cohesion, and tottering under their own *weight*, seem ready to fall before the first blast of the tempest."

    "until these modern days are

"rem prope prolapsam **restituit.**"

"Itaque imperium Aztecanum quo latius patebat, eo fiebat imbecillius; quippe cui ingenti nec convenienter⎱ instituto partes nulla apte⎰ praeditae cohaerendi ratione at⎱ et⎰ magnitudine laborantes⎱ dilabentes⎰ sua prima quaque tempestate iturae essent praecipites."

"donec ad haec tempora quibus

a reached when neither our moral diseases nor their cures are endurable to us."

"these modern days"

See § 4, p. 27, *β*, on "modern developments = haec nova."

"moral diseases"

We must bear in mind that "vitium" is used also of flaws in *β* a building, cp. Cic. *Fam.* 9. 15. 5, and *Top.* 3. 15, "si aedes corruerunt vitiumve fecerunt."

§ 10. "There is one special benefit to be reaped from the study of the past : it is this—the student sees before him lessons of every possible type set in the conspicuous light of historic record; *γ* from these he may gather for himself and his country, examples to imitate, and instances, repulsive from first to last, to avoid."

"There is one special benefit to be reaped from the study of the past; it is this—"

"benefit to be reaped from"— here we have a metaphor familiar *δ* to a nation of husbandmen, who can readily say "a thing beneficial and fruit-bearing," where "to be reaped" is represented by "frugiferum."

So perhaps below in "capere" we have a touch of "gather, reap," cp. "fructus capere, percipere."

"the study of the past"

Here "rerum" gets its colour from the context: it means "re-

nec vitia nostra nec remedia pati possumus, perventum est."

"haec tempora."

"vitia."

"Hoc illud est praecipue in cognitione rerum salubre ac frugiferum, omnis te exempli documenta, in illustri posita monumento, intueri; inde tibi tuaeque reipublicae quod imitere capias, inde foedum inceptu, foedum exitu, quod vites."

"Hoc illud est praecipue in cognitione rerum salubre ac frugiferum,...."

"cognitione rerum."

a rum gestarum." See on § 2, p. 11, β,
"practice = rem."

Next observe the words "There
is one... : it is this—." This is
merely an English idiom for ex-
pressing emphasis.   Put it in
another shape, and we get: "this
is *the* peculiarly beneficial thing."
Now "this is the salutary thing"
β would become in Latin : "hoc est
illud salubre."   Whereas "this is
the salutary thing" will be "hoc
illud est salubre," i.e. "illud" is
separated for stress from "salubre"
to which it properly belongs.

Cp. 5. 2. 3, "this is *the* reason
why it has been decided to pay our
soldiers."

"Hoc illud esse (dictitantes)
quod aera militibus sunt consti-
tuta."

γ   Moreover the "thing is *peculiarly* beneficial," and the stress
on "peculiarly" is expressed
through separating "praecipue"
from "salubre" by the words "in
cognitione rerum."

"it is this—"

Notice the dash.   English
starts a new sentence: "the stu-
δ dent sees," etc.: Latin writes an accusative with infinitive explanatory
of "hoc." Livy could also have
written "hoc illud est...ut omnis
...intuearis," i.e. "*ut* explanatory."
But Latin would rarely have em-
ployed the paratactic form of the
English. (Cp. however Cic. *Phil.*
2. 32. 78, "habebat hoc omnino
Caesar: quem plane perditum...

α cognorat, hunc in familiaritatem
...recipiebat.")

"the student sees before him
lessons of every possible type set
in the conspicuous light of historic
record;"

         "omnis te exempli documenta,
in illustri posita monumento intueri;"

         "the student"

         "te."

—a generic term, and the fact
that it is generic is best expressed
β by saying "one," i.e. te = $\tau\iota\nu a$.
That "one" is a student, is already
shown by "in cognitione rerum."
In fact "student" is a variety of
the "ornate alias."

For this "te" see Madv. 370,
Obs. 2.

         "every possible type"

         "omnis...exempli."

"omnis" is emphasized by
γ separation. See § 5, p. 32, δ, on
"free of every solicitude = omnis
expers curae."

"set in the conspícuous light
of historic record;"

         "in illustri posita monumento."

Consider the Latin—"illustri"
has stress (a) by separation, (b) by
being prepositive.

These examples are set on a
δ record which is lit up, as it were,
by the conspicuousness of the historical characters. If the words
"conspicuous light" be read in-
telligently, we shall put the intonation on "conspicuous"; that
intonation is translated by the
position of "illustri," while the
word itself suggests "light."

         "historic record"

         "monumento.'

See § 1, p. 10, a, on "history of

a the Roman people = res populi Romani," and § 6, p. 36, γ, "the records of genuine history = incorrupta rerum gestarum monumenta."

    "from these...he may gather"   "inde...capias."
      "from these" = "inde"

Livy is very fond of such adverbs instead of a preposition and demonstrative or relative + noun; β here "inde" stands for "ex his."

    In Book I. alone we have:—

    1. 5. 4, inde = ex agris, 1. 9. 10, eo = ad id spectaculum, 1. 10. 1, eo = ad eum, 1. 18. 5, inde = ex Sabinis, 1. 20. 6, quo = ad quem, 1. 24. 2, ibi = penes eos)(unde = a quibus "on whose side," 1. 32. 6, unde = a quibus "by γ whom," 1. 33. 2, eodem = ad eosdem, 1. 34. 4, quo innupsisset = in quae (neut. pl.), 1. 43. 8, inde = ex hac multitudine, 1. 45. 5, ibi = penes eam civitatem, 1. 47. 3, istic = in te "in your case," 1. 47. 12, unde = ut (final) ab ea fortuna, 1. 49. 5, unde = a quibus "from whom."

δ "for himself and his country"   "tibi tuaeque reipublicae."

    Observe how "tuae" is prepositive. The point is this: the student is to find the moral, and apply it to *himself* and *his own* country.

        "country"   "reipublicae."

Livy is thinking of politics especially. He might have used "civitas" with the same allusion nearly (but see § 11, p. 57, δ, "into

a no state = nec in quam civitatem").
But "patriae" would only have
been emotional, as in "Queen
and country."

"he may gather" = one may
gather.   "capias."

The mood in any case would
be subjunctive of the ideal 2nd
person, but it is also a weak
β jussive, i.e. "one *is to* gather,"
which approaches the concessive.

Below, "imitere" and "vites"
are distinctly jussives, i.e., "which
one *is to* imitate, *is to* avoid."

"examples to imitate"   "quod imitere."
"instances to avoid"   "quod vites."

Note the English variety "ex-
γ amples, instances": Latin prefers
parallelism, therefore "quod...
quod." See p. 59, δ and p. 60, δ.

Observe too the neuter pronoun representing noun of English.
See § 5, p. 33, β, on "from the path
of truth = a vero."

"*and* instances"   "*inde*."

"inde" rhetorical anaphora
δ for "et." See next note.

"repulsive from first to last" "foedum inceptu, foedum
              exitu."

The Latin does not express
verbally "in the middle" as well
as "in the beginning and end,"
but the context makes it clear
that this is the meaning. Such
rhetorical devices as "inde...inde,"
"foedum...foedum" are characteristic of all Latin. Romans wrote
for a listening rather than a

α reading public. English strains less after effect.

    Cp. 3. 32. 2, "a famine destructive to man and beast alike,"

    and see note on § 6, p. 44, δ, "the life and civilization of the past = quae vita, qui mores fuerint."

"fames...foeda homini, foeda pecori."

    "Inceptu" seems only to occur here before Seneca. Livy has else-
β where—3. 44. 1, foedo eventu, 3. 53. 2, initio et exitu rei, 26. 38. 4, cum incepto tum etiam exitu, 35. 12. 12, vel incepto vel eventu.

    § 11. "Still, unless I be deceived by affection for the work I have undertaken, there has never existed a country greater, more moral, or richer in types of no-
γ bility; into no state have greed and voluptuousness made their entrance so late, and nowhere has such honour been paid, and for so long, to plain living and frugality: in fact absence of cupidity was proportioned to absence of its objects."

"Ceterum aut me amor negotii suscepti fallit, aut nulla umquam respublica nec maior nec sanctior nec bonis exemplis ditior fuit, nec in quam civitatem tam serae avaritia luxuriaque immigraverint, nec ubi tantus ac tamdiu paupertati ac parsimoniae honos fuerit: adeo quanto rerum minus, tanto minus cupiditatis erat."

    "still"

"ceterum."

δ   "ceterum" is typical of Livy. It occurs once in Terence, once in Cicero, and otherwise not before Sallust. Gild. and Lodge, § 491, note. Roby, § 2209.

    "unless I be deceived..., there has never existed a country..."

"aut me amor...fallit, aut nulla umquam respublica...fuit."

    Note the form of Latin — "either I am deceived...or there never was...." So in English we say, "I am very much mistaken α or this is so " = " unless I am very much mistaken this is so."

This latter method is equally good Latin, cp. 2. 40. 4, " nisi me frustrantur oculi, mater tibi coniuxque et liberi adsunt."

" I be deceived "   " me amor...fallit."

Observe " me " first, as being the logical subject, and cp. the β above citation 2. 40. 4. See on § 5, p. 30, γ, " our generation has lived to witness = nostra tot per annos vidit aetas."

Also there is stress on " me," because the sense is : " *I* may be deceived by affection for *my own work.*"

" affection *for* the work "   " amor negotii."

γ   Cp. § 5, p. 28, δ, on " reward *for* labours = laboris pretium."

" there has never existed a country greater, (or) more moral."   " nulla umquam respublica nec maior nec sanctior...fuit."

We can say : " never a man," but Latin avoids " nunquam quisquam " for reasons of euphony, and prefers " nemo umquam." So here " nulla umquam " not δ " numquam ulla."

" greater, (or) more moral "   " nec maior nec sanctior."

A Roman can split up an original negative (here " nulla ") in two ways : either by " nec... nec " or " aut...aut."

Thus " no one either escaped or lay in hiding " = " nemo $\left.\begin{array}{c}\text{nec}\\\text{aut}\end{array}\right\}$ fugit $\left.\begin{array}{c}\text{nec}\\\text{aut}\end{array}\right\}$ latuit." Here the two α preceding aut's make "aut...aut" impossible for a writer who desires clearness.

[Latin, when it adds a fresh negative, normally contradicts the one preceding, e.g. "non modo non"=not only not; "non nemo" =some people; "non numquam" =sometimes, etc. But the above β is an exception, and also ne... quidem following a negative, e.g. "nemo ne stultus quidem talia facit"=no one, even a fool, acts like this.]

3. 11. 6. "nemo non...non" is rare for "nemo neque (aut)... neque (aut)."

"or richer in types of nobility"   "nec bonis exemplis ditior."

γ   "bonis," prepositive, has stress, i.e. "good")("bad." It keeps up the list: "maior...sanctior," and the whole phrase "nec bonis exemplis ditior" is an adornment of "melior."

"into no state..."   "nec in quam civitatem...."

Observe that English makes an entirely fresh start: the sentence is getting too long. Latin, δ however, combines it closely with the preceding words and in the same form. Indeed one may suspect that Livy first wrote: "nec in quam (sc. rempublicam) tam serae," etc., and then inserted "civitatem" because of the evil-sounding "quam tam."

Of course, as Weissenborn says, "civitatem" may, as usual, refer α more particularly to the state as made up of individual citizens,)(respublica = the state as a whole, as an institution.

 "voluptuousness"   "luxuria."
i.e. the disposition to indulgence)(luxury § 12, p. 60, β = luxus, the indulgence itself.

 "made their entrance so láte"   "tam serae...immigraverint."
β Here "so late" is *the* point, and therefore, having stress, comes early.

Notice the adjective of Latin representing an adverb or the like in English (Madv. § 300, b, c, and Obss. 1 and 2.).

 Cp. 1. 4. 6, "the beast so   "eam adeo *mitem* praebuisse
gently offered her teats."   mammas."
γ 1. 7. 1. "Rĕmus *first*, so the   "*priori* Rĕmo augurium venisse
story goes, received a sign."   fertur."
 1. 16. 2. "Carried up *to heaven*   "*sublimem* raptum procella."
by the whirlwind."
 1. 25. 6. "The Roman troops   "Romanas legiones iam spes
were now *utterly* disheartened."   *tota*...deseruerat."
 1. 31. 4. "The voice *from*   "voce *caelesti* ex Albano monte
heaven on the Alban mount."   missa."
 "nowhere has such honour   "nec ubi tantus ac tamdiu
δ been paid and for so long to   paupertati ac parsimoniae honos
plain living and frugality:"   fuerit:"

The words "paupertati ac parsimoniae" are inserted between "tantus" and "honos" as if complementary genitives, vid. § 3, p. 19, δ, on "in such a cloud of historical witnesses = in tanta scriptorum turba." Indeed, but for the intervening words, the stress on "such" and "so long" would be sacrificed.

α   "plain living"   "paupertas."

A "pauper" is not a beggar (egens), nor is "paupertas" poverty (egestas).

Cp. Cic. *Parad.* 6. 1. 45, " Ista paupertas *vel potius* egestas ac mendicitas."

The two words "pauper" and "paupertas" merely imply humble

β circumstances.

"in fact absence of cupidity   "adeo quanto rerum minus, was proportioned to absence of   tanto minus cupiditatis erat." its objects."

One cannot translate "was proportioned" by a verb (any more than "absence" by a noun); but the *idea* is readily expressed in Latin by quo...eo, quanto...

γ tanto, with comparatives (Greek ὅσῳ...τοσούτῳ). The noun "absence" becomes the verb-phrase. Thus the *meaning* will be: "the fewer were the objects, the less was the cupidity." What is the Latin for objects? "res" will do, for the context clearly decides its force, vid. § 2, p. 11, β, "prac-

δ tice = rem." Notice further that English says: "the *fewer* the objects...the *less*...." But Latin requires no such variety; and "the less" suffices in both cases. Cp. § 10, p. 54, β, on "*examples* to imitate...*instances* to avoid = quod imitere...quod vites."

Thus we get in mere words : "quanto minus rerum, tanto minus cupiditatis erat." But read the

α English, and you find upward intonation at "objects" and "cupidity." We therefore put "rerum" in front of "minus" (i.e. make it prepositive), letting "cupiditatis" go after "minus" to point the antithesis chiastically. Hence Livy's order: "quanto rerum minus, tanto minus cu-
β piditatis erat."

"in fact"   "adeo."

"adeo"=so true is it that, to such an extent is it that.

§ 12. "But of late wealth has brought greed in its train, while unstinted means of enjoyment have introduced a passion for wasting oneself and everything
γ else in the path of luxury and excess.

"nuper divitiae avaritiam et abundantes voluptates desiderium per luxum atque libidinem pereundi perdendique omnia invexere."

Yet criticisms, painful enough, even when they, perhaps, come to be necessary, should at least be unheard at the commencement of this great task."

"sed querelae, ne tum quidem gratae futurae, cum, forsitan, necessariae erunt, ab initio certe tantae ordiendae rei absint."

"But of late..."   "nuper."

"But" is translated by adver-
δ sative asyndeton. Cp. §9, p. 42, δ, on "rather I would have each give...."

"wealth has brought greed... while...means of enjoyment have introduced a craving..."

"divitiae avaritiam et...voluptates desiderium...invexere."

First note "brought" and "introduced." Cp. p. 54, β. One word suffices in Latin: there is no real difference between the two expressions and, moreover, Latin *can wait for its verb.* Now observe the α words "divitiae avaritiam..."—an Englishman *must* have a verb: the Roman need not. He has got the most important facts, viz. that wealth acted in some way *upon* greed—this is shown by the accusative case. He can therefore easily wait for the complete sense, i.e. for the close of the period. Indeed,

β in Latin, the subject and object or objects very frequently come together at the commencement of a sentence, thus at once telling the reader, in the rough, the whole story which follows. Cp. Cic. *Off.* 3. 22. 86, "*Hunc Fabricius* reducendum curavit," and *T. D.* 5. 39. 115, "*Polyphemum Homerus......*

γ cum ariete colloquentem fecit."

"while unstinted means of enjoyment."

"et abundantes voluptates."

*   "while"="et"

Beware of this "while" in English. It either expresses antithesis (Greek δέ) or, as here, is a mere variety for "and" (also δέ).

"unstinted"

"abundantes."

δ There is slight stress on "abundantes" prepositive. Not pleasures are harmful, but too much (abundantes) of them.

"a passion for wasting oneself and everything else in the path of luxury and excess."

"desiderium per luxum atque libidinem pereundi perdendique omnia...."

First observe the order. We have a noun (passion), an attribute (for wasting, etc.) and a comple-

<hr>

* The authors of the *King's English* (p. 357) will have none of this "while" except in contrasts.

α ment (in the path of luxury, etc.). In such cases the complement lies always between the noun and the attribute, and more often than not the attribute comes first. Cp. on § 3, p. 19, δ, "in such a cloud of historical witnesses."

         "in tanta scriptorum turba."

     1. 3. 8. "The name in vogue among succeeding generations."

         "celebre apud posteros nomen."

     1. 4. 6. "Water of little depth **β** on the parched ground."

         "tenuis in sicco aqua."

In the present instance the noun comes first because Livy thereby preserves parallelism. He has written "divitiae avaritiam" and therefore also wishes to write "voluptates desiderium," in order that we may feel at once that "desiderium" is parallel to "ava- **γ** ritiam," and therefore the object of the verb.

     "passion *for* wasting"

         "desiderium...pereundi."

Cp. § 5, p. 28, δ, on "reward *for* labours = laboris pretium."

     "in the path of luxury"

         "per luxum."

"in the path of" is a conventional metaphor, almost dead (cp. § 5, p. 33, β, "from the path of truth **δ** = a vero"). We merely think of it as a less direct way of saying "by luxury"; only it implies "through the agency of" (διὰ + genit.) rather than "directly by" (ὑπό).

Such phrases as "per luxum" are also frequent in Livy as mere varieties for adverbs. Cp. Greek μετ᾽ εὐτελείας = εὐτελῶς, and 1. 5. 2, "half-naked youths were to run about *with jest and gibe*."

         "nudi iuvenes ... per lusum atque lasciviam currerent."

α 1. 5. 5. "But he had been unwilling for the secret to be divulged early *unless a favourable opportunity offered or circumstances made it necessary*."

"sed rem immaturam nisi aut per occasionem aut per necessitatem aperire noluerat."

1. 11. 1. "The army, *seizing the opportunity which the undefended country afforded*, took the offensive and made an inroad into
β Roman territory."

"exercitus per occasionem ac solitudinem hostiliter in fines Romanos incursionem fecit."

1. 11. 5. "*Resentment and greed played no part* in their action."

"nihil enim per iram aut cupiditatem actum est."

1. 41. 6. " *Under pretence of* discharging the functions of another, he strengthened his own position."

"per speciem alienae fungendae vicis suas opes firmavit."

1. 48. 2. "You have been playing your *reckless* game of insult to your masters long enough."

"satis illum diu per licentiam eludentem insultasse dominis."

γ Observe that Livy uses " per " in many senses of παρά, e.g. (1) "during" 3. 29. 7, etc., (2) "on account of" 3. 6. 9, etc., (3) "contrary to" 1. 9. 13, (4) "along" 44. 5. 3.

"yet criticisms, painful enough even when..."
          "criticisms"

"sed querellae, ne tum quidem gratae futurae cum...."
          "querellae."

δ Latin always has a stronger word than English. Thus "dislike" becomes " odium," and " opposition " (e.g. in the senate) is " convicium," etc.

"painful enough even when " = "not pleasant even when "; and Latin with its love of anticipatory words (see § 6, p. 36, *a, β,* on "better fitted") writes: "ne *tum* quidem gratae futurae *cum*...."

a   "perhaps"   "forsitan."

There is no need to regard this as "forsitan" with the indicative. The word may be taken parenthetically as "perhaps" in English.

"they come to be necessary"   "necessariae erunt."

English with equal ease could say: "*are* necessary"; but the event lies in the future, as β "futurae" shows, and "erunt" it must be in Latin.

"should at least be unheard at   "ab initio certe...absint."
the commencement..."

Here we have stress on "commencement," and therefore Latin starts with "abinitio," and "certe" separates it from its genitive "tantae...rei," thus giving it the requisite emphasis.

γ

"of this great task"   "tantae ordiendae rei."

The Livian pleonasm "ordiendae" after "ab initio," as well as its prepositive position, helps to emphasize Livy's point that complaints at the *outset* of his work are ill-omened.

"task"   "rei."

δ   See § 2, p. 11, β, on "practice = rem."

"should be unheard"   "absint."

lit. "are to be absent"—a weak jussive, i.e. optative.

§ 13. "Much more gladly   "cum bonis potius ominibus
would we have started with omens   votisque et precationibus deorum
that were good, and much more   dearumque, si ut poetis nobis
willingly with prayers and sup-   quoque mos esset, libentius in-
plications to gods and goddesses   ciperemus, ut orsis tanti operis
(had our methods been those of   successus prosperos darent."
the poet), that they might have

α blessed the commencement of a great enterprise with a successful consummation."

I have made no attempt to Anglicize this passage : the thought and method of expression are utterly un-English.

"with omens that were good"   "cum bonis (potius) ominibus."

"that were good" is a some-
β what awkward but English method of emphasizing "good")("bad." Latin translates this by making "bonis" prepositive and separating it from its noun "ominibus." In this way too "potius" itself gets stress, and is slightly more than "*more* gladly"; thus by *position* it translates "*much* more
γ gladly."

"would we have started"   "inciperemus."

The imperfect tense is used because the action is incomplete—the Roman historian is supposed to write his preface first.

English could show the difference between "inciperemus" and "incepissemus" by saying "would
δ we have been starting"; but the form is cumbersome, and sometimes impossible (e.g. "valeret" =would have been being strong) and English leaves the exact sense to be decided by the context.

The point of view of both the imperfect and pluperfect subjunctive in hypotheticals may be present or past, but in the im-

a perfect the action is *incomplete*[1], e.g. "moreretur"="he would have been dying" (now or then); and *complete* in the pluperfect, e.g. "mortuus esset"=" he would have died" (now or then).

"supplication to gods"   "precationibus deorum."

Cp. § 5, p. 28, δ, on "reward for labours=laboris pretium"; for "deorum dearumque" cp. Greek

β τῶν θεῶν πάντων καὶ πασῶν.

"much more willingly"   "libentius."

It seems as if Livy, after the interruption "si ut poetis...esset," was merely picking up "potius" in another form when he writes "libentius" before "inciperemus." We could do without it; but Livy is anxious, even at the expense of

γ pleonasm (cp. § 12, p. 64, γ, "initio ...ordiendae") to make clear his preference. Cp. Plato, *Rep.* 1. 346 B.

"had our methods been those of the poet."   "si ut poetis nobis quoque mos esset."

"quoque"=Greek apodotic καί. Thus the above clause would become—(εἰ οἷα τοῖς ποιηταῖς) τοιαῦτα καὶ ἡμῖν προσῆκεν.

δ "that they might have blessed the commencement of a great enterprise with a successful consummation."   "ut orsis tanti operis successus prosperos darent."

Here the antithesis — commencement)(consummation—is reproduced by parallel order, i.e. orsis+epithet)(successus+epi-

---

[1] In fact any possible meaning of the imperfect indicative may be expressed by the "incomplete impossible." See Duff's *Juvenal*, 4. 85.

α thet. Livy might have written a chiasmus, e.g. "orsis tanti operis prosperos successus darent." But it is quite possible that to Livy "prosperos darent" sounded as one word=make prosperous, prosper. So often in poetry, e.g. *Aen.* 1. 63, laxas...dare habenas =laxare; *Aen.* 3. 69, placataque venti dant maria=placare; *Aen.* 9. 323, haec ego vasta dabo =vastabo.

β   "that they might have blessed ...with."   "ut...darent."

The phrase merely *means* "might have given to"—therefore "ut...darent."

The construction may be: (*a*) "ut final," and "darent," partly "final," partly the apodosis of an incomplete impossible=ἵνα ἐδίδο-

γ σαν "in order that they might have been giving."

Cp. 44. 42. 9, quod si maturius pugnari coeptum esset, *ut* satis diei victoribus ad persequendum *superesset*, deletae omnes copiae forent, where "ut superesset" =ἵνα περιεγίγνετο.

Cp. also 26. 49. 14.

δ   But (*b*), no doubt, "darent" is also part of the "precationes"; in which case it is dependent optative, and the sense will be: "I would much sooner have asked the gods to give a prosperous consummation." Then "darent" is naturally attracted into the imperfect by "inciperemus."

INDEX TO CHAP. III.

(The references are to pages and sections)

Printed in the United States
By Bookmasters